Presenting The Palace Past

Other Books by Jim Vaughan

Shapes in Words

Millennium Circus

The Glastonbury Tales

Coalslack and Custard
(Deposited in the Ibstock Time Capsule
and Leicestershire, Leicester and Rutland Record Office)

Presenting The Palace Past

Patrons' Reminiscences of Ibstock Palace Cinema

Compiled
by
Jim & Brenda Vaughan

Published by James Vaughan

Date of Publication
2001

© Jim & Brenda Vaughan 2001

A Catalogue copy for this book is
available from the British Library

ISBN 09533051 2 0

Permission to produce any part or the whole
of this book should be sought
from the Publisher at Logres, Ibstock, LE67 6NR.

Published for The Palace Arts Centre Ltd.

Printed by
ProPrint
Riverside Cottages
Old Great North Road
Stibbington
Peterborough PE8 6LR

Contents

Introduction	1
History, Anecdotes and Extracts	2
Contributions by:	
William H. Dawson	22
Don Clark	27
Ruth Ball	30
Interview with Neville and Adelaine Saunt	32
Maureen Hunter talks on tape	48
Barbara Webster	52
Norman Tomlin	55
Anne Mears	56
Paul Smith	57
Elsie and Gordon Smith	59
Margaret Bills	60
Frieda Taberner	61
Alan Matterson	63
Jim Vaughan	68
'Bid' Wilson	79
A Delve Into The Mercury Archives	81
Appendix	85

Acknowledgements

Permission to reproduce passages from *The Ibstock I Remember, 1910* and *Ibstock, A Story of Her People* by the late L. S. Eggington has kindly been granted by his family.

We have taken the liberty of quoting from the 1938 booklet *Ibstock, A Story of a Leicestershire Village* by Annie Armson, MA, Oxon.

We thank *The Leicester Mercury* and *Coalville Library* for making available their archival material.

Cartoons: Drawn by Adam Bowley.

Cover and Title: Suggested by Don Clark.

Cover Designed by ProPrint.

We are indebted to Derrick Palmer for checking the manuscript. His advice was invaluable. Responsibility for any errors remaining is the compilers'.

JAVBAV, July 2001

The Palace Deteriorating, 25th November 1995
(Photo by The Leicester Mercury)

Restoration Begins, 1998 - 1999
(Photo by Barry Holman)

Presenting The Palace Past

Introduction

The preliminary work on a book of memories about Ibstock Palace Cinema was begun for the Management Committee of the Palace Arts Centre Ltd by the late Donald Mears. When the present compilers agreed to complete the task, Don's material, apparently among papers handed on before his death, could not be found in either the files of the initial application for a building grant on behalf of the Palace Arts Centre Ltd or the archives of the Ibstock Historical Society. Thus, apologies are offered to any of Don's contributors whose work has not been included.

Through a publicity campaign of posters, letters, articles in *The Grapevine*, face to face entreaties, and via the Palace Arts Centre's web-site, the compilers appealed for contributions. Those who submitted written and oral articles provided reminiscences with maximum authenticity. A number of villagers had memories and stories, about which they were prepared to chat, but which they preferred to appear as edited reports. Others passed on information, but had no wish to set down their memories or to have their authorship acknowledged. We thank them all.

Presenting The Palace Past

History, Anecdotes And Extracts

Dating and Ownership

It is believed that the Palace was one of the first purpose-built cinemas[1] in the country. For months, we were unable to determine the precise date of its completion, for reliable documentary evidence eluded us, and human memory is anything but infallible.

One problem of tracing the early history of the Palace stems from the fact that the building was never owned by those who managed the cinema, as the site was leased from the brewery associated with the Ram Hotel, which (when Ibstock Parish Council purchased the Palace to convert to an Arts Centre) was Bass Holdings Ltd. Neither the Bass Estates Manager nor their Archivist has been able to trace any record of the building. The Leicester Land Registry Office has no early reference to the building and its ownership; the Registered Title Number LT285751 is dated 20th August 1996. The only references to the Palace to be found in the Leicestershire Record Office are in items from *The Coalville Times;* the earliest dated 12th July 1991. At the office of *The Coalville Times* we were told that their archives existed only as 'hard copy', which we could not explore. A reporter promised to do this for us but this line of investigation proved futile. *The Leicester Mercury* ran a campaign in the nineties in support of the setting up of an Arts Centre; however, they have no archival record before 1969. We were assured that Coalville Library's archives only went back to 1982. Months later we found that they began much earlier. Although Mr & Mrs Neville Saunt proved most informative, their tenure only ran from 1958.

---

[1] Mr Neville Saunt states that it was built as a theatre. (see interview)

An additional complication, which has led to a fallacious oral tradition, comes about through a number of name changes of Company titles containing the appellation *Bass*. What eventually became Bass Holdings Ltd was in 1888 Bass, Ratcliffe and Gretton. However, at this time the site of the future cinema was owned by James Eadie the Elder, a brewer of Burton upon Trent. At his death on 4th March 1904 it passed to James Eadie, John Thomas Clarke Eadie and William Stewart Eadie. On 15th May 1913 it was conveyed to James Eadie Ltd, whose property it remained until 30th June 1967, when it was conveyed and assigned to Bass Worthington Ltd. Between 1969 and 1978 the latter Company traded as Bass Ltd. In 1978 there was a further name change to Bass Holdings Ltd. About the time that the Parish Council bought the Palace in 1995, the Ram Hotel became the property of Punch Taverns Ltd.

The Site

In the 'gay nineties' the people enjoyed the novelty of a travelling theatre. Every year the well known Mr 'Billy' Holloway erected his portable theatre just off High Street and inside, in an atmosphere warmed by a primitive brazier, the people of Ibstock were moved to tears or laughter by the old favourites of melodrama, *East Lynn*, *Maria Marten*, *The Mormon's Bride*, and *Home Sweet Home*.

Annie Armson
Ibstock, The Story of a Leicestershire Village (1938), p. 16

Mrs Vera Hammonds (née Abell) recalls that the travelling theatre used a barn. Their leading actor, Basil Ray, lodged at the house of Mr & Mrs Len Heath on the west side of

Melbourne Road almost opposite the top of Gladstone Street. She wonders if Billy Holloway was Stanley Holloway's dad.

The late Mr L. S. Eggington in his *The Ibstock I Remember, 1910,* after listing a number of business houses on the south-eastern side of High Street from the corner of Chapel Street towards where the Palace now stands, reported:

> Next was Carter's Cycle Shop and repair room (sic). Mr Moreton's shop stuck out into the street like a sore thumb, backed by a wooden fence up to the Ram Inn gate. The Ram, under Mrs Palmer, put on the best lunches in the district - according to travellers' tales.

In his *Ibstock, A Story of Her People*, Mr Eggington wrote:

> ......then George Moreton's sweet shop. He lost his leg in a mine accident and had a wooden leg which he strapped on. A cheerful character. Behind the fence up to the Ram yard was where the week-end market was, also the site for Billy Holloway's Theatre and Cinema show. There were no seats, the floor went up in tiers of steps. The ground behind was the cricket ground for the town cricket club.

The Building and the Builders

Mr Sim Woolley tells us that Walter Wain, a previous occupant of his bungalow, built the cinema. His brother Bertie was a well-known local architect. Some years ago, their sister, Millie, who was a friend of the late Miss Molly Newman, while staying at Cooper's, asked to look round the bungalow. Mr & Mrs Barry Simpson believe that their grandfathers, Mr Tom Simpson and Mr Ben Baxter, joined forces to erect the building. Mr W. H. Dawson confirms this.

Mr Eggington again:
> If we continue along Station Road we arrive at the bungalow of Walter Wain. He was the founder with his brother Bert, an architect, of the Ibstock Cinema in High Street. Walter was the projectionist when it first opened...... They, along with their parents, were the founders of Wain's brickyard. You can often pick up an old brick with Wain embossed in the frog. Bert Wain and Goddard of Coalville designed the War Memorial in Central Avenue.
>
> L. S. Eggington
Ibstock, A Story of Her People, p.16

Mrs Vera Hammonds reports that 'Butcher' Crane's daughter, Dorothy, who lives at the shop opposite the Ram, believes that the Baxters built the Palace in 1910 and that it opened in 1911. These dates conflict with Mr Eggington's memory:

> In 1912-1913 the Palace was built by Baxter's Builders in High Street. This was a great thrill for us kids. A matinee was run on Saturday afternoons - two pence to go in and a penny nougat from Moreton's basket. He used to come in the Palace with his basket loaded with all kinds of fruit and sweets by kind permission of Mr Wain, the proprietor.
>
> L. S. Eggington
The Ibstock I Remember, 1910, p.16

Presenting The Palace Past

Documentary evidence implies that the Palace did not exist before the spring of 1913. Among the Title Deeds to the Palace is an indenture dated 15th May 1913, an extract of which reads:

> The Vendors (James Eadie, John Thomas Clarke Eadie and William Stewart Eadie) as Trustees hereby convey unto the Company (James Eadie Ltd) that piece of land situate and fronting to High Street in the Parish of Ibstock and County of Leicester containing Five hundred square yards or thereabouts bounded on the North or Northwesterly side thereof by the High Street on part and by a lock-up shop now (*as* ?) formerly belonging to and in the occupation of John Thomas Lawrence in the other part on the South or Southwesterly side thereof by the Cricket Field on the East or Southeasterly side thereof by hereditaments belonging to the Company and on the West or Southwesterly side thereof by the yard appurtenant to the Ram Hotel belonging to the Company which piece or parcel of land hereby conveyed comprises the site of four messuages cottages or tenements with gardens and other appurtenances thereto belonging conveyed to the said to James Eadie the Elder by an Indenture of Conveyance dated 26th March One thousand nine hundred and made between Mary Ann Stone Andrew of the one part and the said James Eadie the Elder of the other part and which said messuages and buildings have been pulled down and removed (*To hold the same* --?) unto and to the use of the Company and its assigns for ever.
>
> (For this piece of land £310.00 was paid.)

Since the lock-up shop predates the Palace, Mr Barry Simpson wonders if anyone can confirm that Mr George Moreton (or later his son Herbert) had a stake in the Palace project.

The Opening

When Derrick Palmer received the manuscript to check, he immediately resolved the problem of the date of the opening of The Palace. By visiting Coalville Library, he confirmed his conviction that early copies of *The Coalville Times* are indeed held there on micro film. He produced the following extract dated 3rd January 1913:

Ibstock Picture Palace

The above picture house is situated in the High Street, adjoining the 'Ram' Hotel. It is a substantial brick building occupying a site nearly 500 square yards. There are two main entrances, leading to the hall direct from High Street, having an imposing effect, being carried out in massive facing brick *pillastres* (sic) and concrete dressings with ramped concrete parapet over main entrance, the whole of the external walls being built in 14 in. brickwork. The main hall is 72ft 6in. long and 30ft 5in. wide. In addition to this, a balcony 36ft by 14ft is erected at one end and at the other a raised stage, 29ft wide by 18ft deep, with dressing rooms at either side having a private staircase leading to same. The engine-house and emergency staircase from balcony is erected at the rear of the hall, also three emergency exits fitted up with automatic panic bolts. The whole of the hall is fitted with tip-up seats, those to the balcony being upholstered in red plush; the floor of the balcony being carpeted to match. The stage front has an imposing feature, being carried out in moulded wood *pillastres (sic),* and large cornice at the top, the opening being 18ft by 12ft 3 in. There is seating accommodation for 650. The whole of the walls are colour-washed down to the wood dado in deep rich red, the ceiling, stage, and balcony front, being relieved in white. All the other internal woodwork is a dark brown, varnished. The hall is well ventilated by fresh air inlets, and large extract ventilators at ridge. The whole of the picture hall is lighted throughout with electricity, supplemented by gas, if required. The front of the palace, over the entrance is illuminated by electric lights. The hall has a sloping floor, giving each person a clear view of the stage. The hall is heated by radiating stoves, and ample fire appliances are provided in different parts of the hall. The operating box is built in brick at rear, with iron roof. The company has spared no expense in erecting this hall to provide a comfortable and substantial building for the public.

The architects for the building were Messrs Goddard and Wain, Coalville, and the builder Mr B. Baxter of Ibstock. Mr V.T. Simpson of Ibstock carried out the woodwork, and Mr C.H. March of Coalville the decorating and plumbing.

The Palace was opened on Boxing Day, an excellent programme being given, and there have been large audiences.

Presenting The Palace Past

An Article from the Same Edition

PICTURE PALACE, IBSTOCK

The above commodious picture palace, recently opened, is being well-patronised, and Ibstockonians are now being well-catered for in the way of amusement, which will no doubt be much appreciated.

We would call Ibstock readers' attention to the excellent tariff arranged for next week. Amongst other items may be mentioned 'The wheel of destruction,' a very exciting piece; 'The cry of children,' a film illustrating the hardships of mill life; a Gaumont drama 'The old Chateau,' (coloured); 'The flooded mine,' one which should appeal specially to patrons in this district. The length of this film is 2,500ft and (it) is a very exciting piece. This should be seen. There are also some very good comics. Some excellent music is also discoursed during the evening, and a most instructive and comfortable evening may be spent at a reasonable charge. Full particulars as to times and prices of admission may be seen in our advertisement columns.

Presenting The Palace Past

PALACE

IBSTOCK

JANUARY 6th and during the Week
MONDAY to FRIDAY inclusive,
Once nightly at 7.30.
Early Doors. 1d. extra at 7.
Ordinary Doors at 7.15

SATURDAY (Two Houses) at 6.30 and 8.30.
Early Doors at 6 and 8.15.
Ordinary doors at 6.15 and 8.20

CHILDREN'S MATINEE on SATURDAY at 2.30;
Doors open at 2;   1d. and 2d.;
Adults: Usual price

PICTURES
Monday, Tuesday and Wednesday

THE BARRIER THAT WAS BURNED
(Thrilling Vitagraph Drama)
WHEEL OF DESTRUCTION
(1,435 feet of absolute excitement)
WARWICK CHRONICLE
(Illustrating the World's Happenings)
TEDDY OBJECTS TO SMOKE
(A yell from start to finish)
THE CRY of the CHILDREN
(Magnificent subject showing the hardships of the
Mill-workers)

Presenting The Palace Past

<u>Thursday, Friday and Saturday</u>

TWILIGHT
Very pathetic drama, will appeal to young and old alike.

THE OLD CHATEAU
(Fine coloured French drama by Gaumont Co.)

THE ELECTRIC BELT
(This will make you Scream)
Regardless of great cost we have secured an exciting drama that will interest local patrons.

THE FLOODED MINE
This picture is 2,500ft long, and depicts the horrors of a mine flooded while the men are down. See the thrilling rescue when all hope has been abandoned.

Special Notice. For the benefit of our patrons who work on the night shift, we have decided to have a Matinee every Tuesday Morning. Doors open 10; commence at 10.30.

Entire Change of Programme every Monday and Thursday.

Popular Prices:
Balcony 9d., Children 6d.;
Pit Stalls 4d., Children 2d.;
Pit 3d., Children 2d.
Seats may be reserved on the Balcony at a small charge of 3d.
Early Doors 1d. extra to all parts.
No money returned.

Manager   Mr G W White.

Presenting The Palace Past

Early Days of the Cinema

Few alive today can remember that during the First World War the building was used as a recruiting centre, but we are yet again indebted to Mr Eggington's *The Ibstock I Remember, 1910,* p.16:

> On the outbreak of War recruiting meetings were held at the Palace. Capt. Stevenson used to come with several men. Any volunteers received the King's Shilling and they were in the Army. I well remember the scene at home when my brother Tom and his cousin had joined up at the Palace. This was 1915. He was back in England wounded before the year was out. I remember Dickie Pepper Gray - the town crier - coming round the streets announcing a special meeting at the Palace at 7 o'clock Sunday night. Mr Dunstan read out Sir Douglas Haig's telegram to the troops 'Back to the Wall. Not one more yard must be yielded. Every position must be held to the last man. This was Germany's final throw, an attempt to break through to the Channel ports. Britain's contemptible little army held the line.' The same message was sent by Marshall Foch to the French troops holding Verdun. They chalked on the walls of the town 'C'est Ne Pas' (They shall not pass). *(sic)* [2]

Many people tell us that Mr Alty Adcock played the piano to accompany the silent films. Mr Jack Newman of High Street

---

[2] The war-cry was: 'Ils ne passeront pas.' - *Editor*

Presenting The Palace Past

'Any volunteers received the King's Shilling….and they were in the Army.'

Presenting The Palace Past

'When the tree fell, the plank was supposed to fall. It did, and brought the screen down.'

adds that his aunt, the late Mrs Florence Eleanor Tonks (née Newman) of the 'Tin Shop' also regularly played.

Mr Sim Woolley recalls that about this time, he lived in one of the Colliery Houses. His journey to the Palace took him through the Brickyard along a path much used by the general public in those days. By the Gasworks in Spring Lane, the path ran close to Meadow Row. Sim frequently had fights with lads from there - possibly for the fun of it, because later he became a well-known local amateur boxer.

He tells an amusing tale from the days of silent films. The scene was set in a forest where wood was being chopped. Someone on stage behind the screen was commissioned to make the sound effects by thwacking a plank. When the tree fell, the plank also was supposed to fall. It did, and brought down the screen. Was this the origin of the term *show-stopper?*

Talent Contests, Mrs Vera Hammonds informs us, were held in the late twenties. At the age of twelve or thirteen, her future husband, John, won three old pennies for playing the bones.

The Talkies

In New York on the 6th October 1927 the 'talkies' arrived, The applauding audience was brought to its feet, when in the middle of a night club scene in *The Jazz Singer,* Al Jolson spoke: 'Wait a minute, wait a minute,' he said. 'You ain't heard nothin' yet!'

How soon did the 'talkies' surprise the villagers of Ibstock? According to Neville Saunt, Barlestone had talking pictures by around 1931. Mrs Vera Hammonds recalls that Ibstock's first 'talkie' was *High Society Blues*, starring Janet Gaynor.

The Thirties

One of Mr Don Middleton's early memories is of the cowboy star Tom Mix, for whom John Wayne did odd jobs. It is alleged that Tom Mix promised the 'Duke' a job in films, but failed to give him the figurative leg up he had been promised.

The programme at the Palace did not always consist of films. Was it a Restoration piece that prompts the memory of piled white wigs, a predominance of orange and yellow costumes touched with green, and of strutting actors and high-backed chairs? The date must have been the early thirties.

Between the Wars the British Legion Gala Queen was crowned and Fancy Dress competitors were judged on the stage.

Mr Jack Newman reminds us that, from the thirties to the post-war period, an occasional lecturer to visit the Palace was his father's cousin Bernard Newman, the novelist. He gave illustrated accounts of his tours of many countries through which he travelled on George, the faithful bicycle that he seemed to regard as his companion. During the Second World War, he was an official lecturer for the Ministry of Information. He also fulfilled similar engagements in Ashby de la Zouch town hall, where in addition to the general public he sought to stir patriotism in the hearts of the senior boys of the Boys' Grammar School. In Ibstock the cul-de-sac *Bernard Close* bears his name.

Presenting The Palace Past

By this time the upper ticket office of the Palace was the domain of Beatrice Mattley, who lived at 142 Melbourne Road by the corner with the 'Black Path'. The lower ticket office was in the capable hands of Mrs Maud Clark. At some time Ivy Adcock of Heather worked in the office. Two part-time projectionists were 'Smart' Flamson and Harry Gilliver.

Public performances were often punctuated by extraneous noises. The thwack of leather on willow from the summer cricketers in the Ram field was augmented by the sound of appreciative applause. At the time of the Parish Church's Patronal Festival in October, the wild cries from the Heyday Skidders, the Noah's Ark, the Dodg'ems, and the Swingboats, coupled with the deep throbbing of the traction engines, generating power, shattered the romantic peace of the moonlit silver screen.

It is surprising how small a part music seems to have played in these recorded memories. Most, but not all, children in the thirties greeted the short big band films, which were often sandwiched between comedies - featuring such favourites as The Three Stooges, The Keystone Cops, or Buster Keaton - and the main film, with the same derision that greeted soft-focus mushy kissing. Yuk! Few were aware that *The Grand National* and *The Derby* were invariably run against a background of Ponchielli's *The Dance of the Hours*, or that the Red-skins were encouraged in their chase of the stagecoach by the tumultuous strains of Mendelssohn's *Hebrides Overture*.

The Forties

During the Second World War, hedge-hopping R.A.F. planes strafed Northern Europe accompanied by Maestro R. Vaughan

Presenting The Palace Past

'..the Red-skins were encouraged...by the music...'

Presenting The Palace Past

'…..derision greeted soft-focus mushy kissing…'

Williams and a swarm of his *Wasps*. Patriotism was also fostered among those who remained for the whole of *The National Anthem* by encouraging them to march to the exits to the stirring measures of one of Sir Edward Elgar's *Pomp and Circumstance* marches, or Sir William Walton's *Crown Imperial*.

Perhaps music made a limited impact for the very reason that good film music is that which is not consciously registered. After all the true impact of film is the image, which has resulted in momentous social changes, unforeseen in 1938 when Annie Armson, in her booklet, chose to make no mention of the Palace. Did she regard it as a den of iniquity?

Mr Walter Fowkes tells us that, during the Second World War, his father frequently ferried Mr Richard Edward Ball, the lease-holder, from and to Earl Shilton, because Mr Ball's petrol ration was limited, whereas Mr Harry Fowkes had an extra allocation to run his taxi service.

The Fifties and Later

Mr Anthony Lawrence, formerly of Station Road, writes from Otago, New Zealand, that he recalls with pleasure Saturday morning film shows, when an old sixpence gained him admission to see such treasures as *Robin Hood* - with Richard Green, *Davy Crockett,* and *Jailhouse Rock.* Mr Gerald Chamberlain, who annually delighted in watching the fun-fair traction engines and lorries squeezing through the gap between the Ram and the cinema, also recalls Saturday morning film shows, a memory shared by Mr Keith Page.

The period from 1958 to 1986 is authentically described by Mr and Mrs Neville Saunt in the transcript of their interview.

Presenting The Palace Past

From 1986 the Palace, inhabited by its own phantoms and ghosts from the past, stood empty. It was soon to be in danger of terminal decline.

Ibstock Parish Council bought the Palace from Bass Holdings Ltd on 3rd October 1995 for the sum of £40,000 plus VAT at the standard rate, a total of £47,000. The lease, at a peppercorn rent, was handed over to Mr Ken Smith, the Chairman of the Palace Arts Centre Ltd, by the Council's Chairman, Councillor Don Costello, on 14th October, 2000.

The impact of these memories taken as a whole is a measure of the significance of the Palace in the life of Ibstock and the surrounding parishes during the twentieth century. . Can it play a similarly valuable role in the New Millennium?

Exterior: c 1950 - 1960 (Source unknown)

Presenting The Palace Past

Mr William H. Dawson Reminisces

*Based on long conversations with him
at his home in Market Bosworth
on the evenings of 9th January and 20th March 2001*

In its early days the Palace was owned, it was understood, by the Wain family of Station Road and built by Ben Baxter and Tommy Simpson. Baxter was the builder, and Simpson was the carpenter. Bert Wain was an architect, and there are many local examples of his expertise, so it can be assumed that he designed and supervised the erection of the Palace. I remember that the Wains had a sister Millie. Sim and Margaret Woolley now live in the bungalow that was once her home.

I am surprised to hear that the site of the Palace was not owned by the Wain family, but was leased from the brewery. I can't imagine them building on land they didn't own, unless of course they had a long lease, ninety-nine years or longer. You will understand why some people get confused about which brewery was involved when I tell you that Bass, Worthington and James Eadie closely co-operated and worked together from the same office area. My father had two horses and a dray with which he carried beer from Heather station to the Ram, the Oak, the Waggon and Horses and the 'Beer-offs': The Retreat on Leicester Road and Milestone House on Melbourne Road.

My boyhood friends included, among many others, Jack Cooper and George Moore. In his boyhood days Jack used to assist in the Palace. He was always modest and in later life was an unsung hero: the fifth man to be chosen for the original S.A.S. He told me that after a raid they would be allowed a few days leave and he always went to his old school to meet

Presenting The Palace Past

'....until the day of retribution.'

Presenting The Palace Past

'....not slow to find a squint hole.'

his headmaster and teachers. Mr Measures, the headmaster, would present him at Assembly to the whole school as an old pupil.

We lads would try all sorts of tricks to get into the cinema without paying. In those days money was scarce. Sometimes it was possible to pass the pay-box and the ticket-tearer under someone's long mack. Another of our ruses, and I suppose others have tried this dodge since, was to arrange for one of our number to buy a ticket for the show. As soon as the lights faded, and the coast being clear, he would go to the toilet exit and, without disturbing the curtains, would carefully ease down the bar to open the door. His fellow conspirators, having climbed over the back boundary wall, would be waiting to sneak in. To scale the wall required lads in turn to be given a leg up and the 'last man' to be hoisted up by his friends on the wall. This ruse had succeeded many times, until the day of retribution arrived and Jack Cooper was met with a bucketful of cold water.

Harry Gilliver, who was projectionist at that time, used to tell roguish tales of visits by groups of travelling players that often included a troupe of chorus girls. As the Palace lacked proper dressing-room facilities, the girls had to make do with any space available - and a bucket. Peeping Toms were not slow to find a squint-hole. I never had the opportunity to squint, but Jack told me that he did.

One of these travelling showmen, who provided a change from the cinematograph, was Basil Ray.

Ellis Mee owned a red *Indian Prince* motorbike, much admired by some of the chorus girls, until the day he took one of their number for a ride in the direction of Tamworth.

Presenting The Palace Past

Unfortunately they had a crash and she never went on his bike again.

This was at a time when the cinema seating consisted of long, splintery benches at the front. Seats in the balcony were better, but a balcony ticket cost nine pence.

Important events in the village and at the Palace were announced by 'Dickie Pepper' Gray, the Town Crier.

'….and she never went on his bike again.'

Don Clark Remembers

My family had always had a close connection with the Palace. Both my mother and father worked there for many years. Without a doubt my mother was the longest serving member of the Palace staff. She worked there from before her marriage to my father until the latter part of her life, when ill-health caused her to quit. My own association with the Palace started at a very early age; at six months old I was parked in my pram in the 'Bottom Office'. The late Rosa Price, bless her, said she could remember seeing me there in a little woolly hat.

No doubt my mother could have told you many stories. I can remember one character named Simon Smith, who, because of my mother's maiden name, used to say to her at the box office: '"The Lord is my *Shepherd.*" Two for the chicken run.' I do not know whether this pleased or annoyed her.

The Managers

The first people I knew were called Wain, who lived at 'Hill Crest,' Heather. They had a daughter Bessie, who must have taken a shine to me because when she holiday'd on the Continent, she used to bring me foreign coins, some of which I still have.

Mr & Mrs Ball

Mr and Mrs Ball of Earl Shilton were the next people I remember as owners. Mrs Ball always seemed a nice lady and Mr Ball was a short, thick-set man with slicked down hair and a bark to rival Sgt Major Brittain. He was a strict disciplinarian; any sign of frivolity or high spirits and he would ring a bell to the projectionist and the film or sound would be cut. Neither would he allow any impropriety, i.e. putting your arm around your girl-friend's shoulder. If you were spotted, his torch would cut through the darkness like a sword of light and pick you out, causing much embarrassment.

Neville and Adelaine Saunt

Neville and Adelaine Saunt I did not know very well. I knew Neville from working at the B.U.S.M.C. Company, Leicester, but I know they received my mum's respect and devotion. During her employment by Mr & Mrs Saunt, Betty and I had to retain safely the Saturday-night's takings until Mum went to work on Monday night.

Perks

I, personally, had a unique privilege because of my mother's staff status; I always had a complimentary ticket, which meant that I could meet my now dear wife inside and thus reduce our courtship budget.

Another perk I had was that I was able to ring Betty at the pictures when I joined the forces. In fact, she was allowed to visit the top office for my call on the night before I embarked to the Middle East, thus enabling us to speak for quite a while before our separation.

Before the birth of our children we were both co-opted to perform tasks like selling and ripping the tickets.

One film that I do remember as a step in my life was *Blues in the Night,* which starred Jack Carson as a wayward trumpet player. It also featured the Jimmy Lunceford Orchestra, which probably spawned my love of Big Swing Bands. So I suppose the Palace played some part in my love of my dear wife and my love of music, they were the good bits. But as a child I sometimes felt like a Palace orphan.

Postscript

I don't remember the 'rope' episode[3], but my dear friend Harry Smith says that he does, as Mr Ball put it there to stop the girls attacking him.

---

[3] See page 53.

Presenting The Palace Past

Mrs Ruth Ball of Earl Shilton
Talks About
Mr Richard E. Ball, her late Father in Law

Mrs Ruth Ball is the widow of Mr Victor Ball. She now lives on part of the site previously occupied solely by the senior Mr and Mrs Ball's house.

Those patrons of the Palace who felt that Mr R. E. Ball was something of a disciplinarian may not be surprised to learn that the first of his several careers was as a teacher at the Church of England School in Earl Shilton. Later he went into partnership with a hosiery manufacturer and they traded as Ball and Minard.

The senior Mrs Ball's maiden name was Cooper and her father owned the Palace Cinema in Earl Shilton. Perhaps this inspired his son-in law to acquire the lease of the Ibstock Palace. Although the running of the cinema occupied their evenings, during the day Mr and Mrs Ball were free to pursue their interest in antiques, in which they both traded and furnished their home.

A few young friends of Victor, who often accompanied his father to see the show, were not the only youngsters to be collected by Mr Ball, who found patrons in at least one of the small neighbouring villages.

During his time at Ibstock, he was unable to show films until they had been exhibited at Coalville. This must have been frustrating for him, but less so for the bus proprietors. Experience taught him that Ibstock folk were not over fond of too many romantic films and love stories, but preferred westerns and exciting adventure films. The popular songs of the day did not appeal to his taste and for incidental music he usually chose marches, which in wartime accorded with the spirit of the day.

Television sets soon began to appear after the war and the shop opposite the cinema had more than most electrical shops in the area. The Coronation gave sales a boost and, as the popularity of television increased, cinema-going began to decline.

Mr R.E.Ball and his House at Earl Shilton (Photo of House: Barry Holman)

An Interview With Neville & Adelaine Saunt
Recorded at their home, 147, Main Street. Newbold Verdon,
24th October 2000
Conducted by Brenda & Jim Vaughan

Players

A: Adelaine Saunt   N: Neville Saunt
B: Brenda Vaughan   J: Jim Vaughan

Reel One

B: I believe that Mr Ball of Earl Shilton owned the Palace before you.

A: Yes. Leasehold.

B: So you bought it from him?

A: No. We leased the cinema from the brewery - Bass - just as Mr Ball had done.

B: And the land has always belonged to the brewery?

N: As far as I know, but that's going back a bit.

B: So you don't know who built the cinema or who was the architect?

A: One lad told us that his dad had helped to build it, but -

N: Wain! Mr Wain.

B: He was the architect?

Presenting The Palace Past

A: No, he was the one who had it built.

J: But there were two Wain brothers; Berty Wain was an architect.

N: It was built in a similar style to the one we had at Shepshed.

A: I don't know when the Palace was built. I can't remember much before Mr Ball finished. I didn't know much about Ibstock.

J: Walter Fowkes has told me that Mr Ball's house at Earl Shilton was most interesting.

N: Yes, Shilton. It was interesting. It might be worthwhile going over and photographing it. It's still there, but I don't know who lives there now. In Mr Ball's day it was known as 'The Mansion.' He collected antiques and the house was filled with them.

J: Walter said that it was like a Hitchcock-

N: Like something out of a Hitchcock movie - very interesting.

B: And when did you take over from Mr Ball?

N: Nineteen-fifty-eight.

B: Till when?

A: I've got it all written down. I ought to....

(She fetches a notebook.

Presenting The Palace Past

N: We were there twenty-eight years.

B: So, that would be eighty-six.

A: Nineteen-eighty-six. Yes, fifty-eight to eighty-six.

B: And how long did you actually show films, because you weren't showing films at the end, were you?

N: Approximately nine years.

A: About nineteen-sixty-three Bingo came in. For a start we ran films and Bingo; we had films some nights and Bingo others. Nobody came to see the films - because of television. We weren't doing very well with films unless we had...... We did best with kiddy films.

B: We've been told that you used to alternate your programmes with the cinema at Barlestone.

N: No, that was Enderby and Barlestone.

B: So while you were at Ibstock did you swop films with anyone?

A: No - we had films just for Ibstock.

J: We've heard also that Mr Ball exchanged films with Barlestone.

N: Not as far as we know.

A: No Barlestone always swopped with Enderby The Chestertons owned and ran Enderby and Barlestone.

Presenting The Palace Past

B: And the 'talkies'?

N: I think Barlestone had the 'talkies' about nineteen-thirty one.

J: Very early. With the expense of new sound projectors?

N: Oh no, just sound heads. They were easily fitted on to the projectors. The sprocket-holes in the films were the same.

J: That wouldn't happen today. Too convenient! Now about the Palace projectionists? Joe Satchwell?

N: That's right. Mr Satchwell was projectionist for Mr Ball and his son gave him some help.

J: That's how my memory works - Jim Satchwell, the father; Joe, the son. But Maureen, Joe's daughter, speaks of Jim as *Uncle* Jim. She must know. She says that they did all the cleaning and always had.

N: That's right, I think, but we don't really know.

A: When we took over Neville showed the films and later on Joe Fowkes helped with the projection. I did some cleaning and booked the films. Oh, I mustn't forget Mrs Clarke, who was in the pay-box for Mr Ball and continued in the pay-box for me because she liked doing it. She was elderly and a treasure as she knew everyone.

J: Her son, Don, spells his name: 'Clark without an "*e*".' Yet somehow I picked up the notion that his father was a distant relation of my maternal grandmother's family and they always spelt their name with an '*e*'.

A: Well I am not sure about an *'e'* as I knew nothing of Ibstock until we actually took over the Palace.

B: So which pay-box did Mrs Clark use? The top or the bottom one?

A: Oh, we only used the one up the steps.

J: That was promotion for her. Beatty Mattley used to be there and Mrs Clark (without an *'e'*) was at the bottom box.

A: She knew everybody. She was quite efficient.

Reel Two

N: So some people want to do the Palace up?

J: Already the Council have had to spend a great deal of money to a 'skip' firm to clear out the old seats.

A: They all came from Ashby when that cinema closed. Their seats were better than ours. I think we got the lot for a tenner.

B: Where was the Ashby cinema?

N: About where Somerfield's is today.

A: Ashby seats were better. In the Palace the balcony seats were best. The front seats were always the worst.

B: But they had the worst treatment, didn't they?

N: Yes.

Presenting The Palace Past

A: Although when we went to Ibstock, the front seats were all wooden and in perfect condition, but worn. The kiddies didn't mind that they weren't soft. They were all shiny.

B: Nobody had carved their names- ?

N: No, they were all right.

A: They were rather nice. I thought, 'Gosh, wooden seats!'

N: They were practical.

B: I can remember sitting on them.

J: Of course now they've all gone. When the firm came to clear the building, one guy climbed on to the stage and shouted to his mates, 'Oy, there's a trapdoor 'ere!' He pulled the bolt and shot through, down to the boiler house.

N: He would do. Yes.

A: That's ever so funny, because one day I went in, put the lights on, looked down to the front - and the trapdoors were down. We'd had burglars in the night. They'd got in, down the stoke-hole, then from underneath the stage. I don't know how they dared.

J: Did they take anything?

A: Not that I could see. There was nothing for them to take - only sweets.

B: Tell me about it being haunted.

N: Being haunted? I've never seen any ghosts there.

Presenting The Palace Past

J: Maureen Hunter, Joe Satchwell's daughter, tells how one day her dad, after unlocking, found a policeman's helmet hanging from the roof. She had been told that there was no ladder in Ibstock long enough to get up there.

N: Oh there was. There was one with the picture house that reached to the girders. It was kept under the stage.

A: Yes, the bulbs didn't last for ever, so you needed one to get up there.

N: They were high.

A; Very, very high.

B: But Maureen reckons it was haunted.

A: Well I used to go in all on my own in the daytime - Neville being at work - to get ready for the evening. I never had any feeling - no, never felt peculiar to me...... It was still a coal boiler when we went, so I used to have to stoke it.

N: We had a gas one put in as soon as we could afford it.

A: I knew a salesman for the Gas Board. and he came and told me what I wanted. As far as I know it's still working.

N: It's still gas now?

B: I don't know. They've taken a lot of stuff out, but even now the place is fantastic. Some art-deco paint is still there, but peeling. It really takes you back.

A: So what are they planning to do with it ?

J: The Committee had a model made to show how it might be developed as an Arts Centre. Very ambitious. There was even to be a tower for flying scenery.

A: Oh I say! I mean Ibstock's Ibstock!

Reel Three

A: There's nothing beyond the wall at the back belonging to the picture house. We always used the ground at the back as a car-park. Although it was owned by the brewery, we always got on with Bernard, who used to be landlord at the 'Ram'.

J: Bernard Houghton?

N: Yes. You remember him?

J: 'Drummer'. We were in the same class at the Junior School.

A: He had a really good business. We never had a drinks licence. The brewery didn't want us in competition. What used to happen was that the men who wanted a drink ordered it and Bernard would have them ready for when they went into the pub during the interval.

J: Bernard's wife was Betty, the daughter of the previous landlord, Sam Underwood.

A: Bernard, yes, he was very outgoing.

J: Can you tell us anything about travelling theatre companies - before the cinema was built or later?

B: We've been told that Billy Holloway's players came regularly.

J: Several people reckon that he was Stanley's father.

N: No, I can't help you. When they cleaned the place out, were there any old photographs there?

B: No one seems to know the whereabouts any of that kind of stuff. Don Mears had collected material and before he died handed it on to-

J: Someone.

B: But it has gone missing. I've asked Stuart Howe, the Chairman of the Historical Society, who was given boxes and boxes by Don, but Stuart is sure that he has nothing connected with the Palace.

N: Didn't they find any posters?

B: No one seems to know.

J: Right. Let's talk about films. Can you remember any you showed?

A: I've all my old film diaries. They're the only things we've kept. We just kept the film books. I'll just-

>*(Adelaine goes to collect a box of diaries.)*

It's all in pencil, actually, because I sometimes wanted to rub it out and alter it. There, that's for 31st March, 1958: *Toy Tiger* and *Outside the Law*. The next: *Miracle in Soho* and *Frances and the Haunted House*. These were all Rank

- Top Rank, but we dealt with nearly every.... MGM., 20th Century Fox....

N: We only slipped up on Paramount; we never had a Paramount.

A: We didn't need them really.

B: And you, like Mr Ball, used to show two programmes a week?

N: Three a week.

A: Because we soon showed every night. *Seven Brides for Seven Brothers* was in April 1958, which was when that film came out - well about then. Obviously we didn't get it immediately. *Hell Drivers* - bet you can remember that. It was a Rank one. *Friendly Persuasion* - MGM.

N: *Square Peg* - Norman Wisdom.

A: No, *Square Jungle; Garden of Eden*. I've got them all down. *High Society* - another top MGM film at the time.

B: I see you have pictures there.

A: Only in the official diaries. That's all I kept. When somebody said that we never had a particular film at Ibstock, because it was too small a place, I could show them. We didn't get them as soon as Leicester and Coalville, but we could get them all.

B: Here's a picture called *Dangerous Exile*, with Belinda Lee and Louis Jourdan.

Presenting The Palace Past

A: That would be Top Rank.

B: And on the other side of the page?

A: *Wisdom's Way* - but that's not Norman Wisdom.

B: Peter Finch and Mary Ure.

A: This is all 1958. *Blackboard Jungle* - you'll remember that one. *Attila the Hun; Guilty* - in the week. *Davy Crockett and the River Pirate.*

J: Which were the last films? We can't just reproduce the whole list.

(They have a discussion about which year they stopped showing films. By 1969 Top Rank had ceased supplying diaries, but Adelaine kept a record in an ordinary notebook.)

A: *On the Beat.*

B: *On the Beach* - Neville Shute?

A: No, *On the Beat* - that would be Norman Wisdom, I think. *Planet of the Apes; Survival;* Elvis Presley - *Speedway.* This is coming towards the end: *Crooks and Coronets; The Golden Goose; Around the World; Play Dirty.*

B: The last film according to this was Tuesday, 23rd December, 1969.

N: Don't forget the matinees.

A: Oh wait! 1st January, 1970: *Jungle Book.* That looks like the last film.

B: So you were showing films for about twelve years.

Reel Four

B: Had you any other cinemas besides Ibstock and Shepshed?

N: No.

B: So you divided your time between Ibstock and Shepshed?

A: Yes.

B: Who was the projectionist?

N: Mr Commons, at Shepshed. Yes, Mr Commons. He's just died. He was showing when we went and continued showing for us.

B: Did you have any other projectionists?

N: Fowkes.

A: Joe Fowkes at Ibstock.

N: Joe came when he was fourteen or fifteen. He didn't work for us when he first came. He just couldn't keep away from the pictures.

A: Mr Hall brought him across. 'I've brought you this nice lad,' he said. 'He's dying to show the pictures.'

N: Joe still comes to see us.

B: Where does he live?

A: Newbold. He's an electrician by trade. He worked for a firm in Coalville, till he set up on his own. This does date the films.

B: How much did it cost to hire a film?

N: It depended on what you took at the box-office. If your takings were down so were their payments. You only paid according to your takings at the box-office.

J: Less Entertainment Tax?

A: Entertainment Tax! Yes, right from day one. There's always been a tax on films. That was my introduction to Customs and Excise when I first went there in 1958. 'What? Tax on films?' You had to keep proper records.

J: Was there a notice about tax printed on the tickets?

N: The tickets were all numbered.

A: I can't remember it specially. I remember the tax-man. He came from Ashby - the local one. But I can't remember having our tickets specially printed with anything about tax on. I can't remember now, but the tax came as a shock.

(We take a short tea-break,
(but longer than the occasional break of a film.

B: I find these diaries interesting. I see there's a list here that you could choose from.

A: No, salesmen came round to see us.

N: Twentieth Century Fox came to your house.

A: And you bought so many programmes at a time - probably for about three months. There was no such thing as: 'You can have this and you can have that.' You got a list. The popular films you didn't get as quickly as the bigger cinemas. The first run and the second run, but there's hardly a second run left. I can remember when 'the chariot thing' came in, you had to wait a long time for that. They'd get it at the big Ranks and the Odeons.

N: Ben Hur!

A: They kept that on for about three months.

N: We never did show it. When they told us we could have it, we didn't want it. Everybody had seen it.

J: So you had wide-screen?

N: We did have wide-screen, oh yes. We had Cinemascope.

J: I'd forgotten, but after about 1959 we almost stopped going to the cinema.

N: Everybody did. Television.

A: Cinemascope. Yes, we had it all the way round. It was a different....

B: Shape?

A: You opened the screen out for Cinemascope.

J: Someone, who claims to know a lot about the Palace, reckons that the screen is still there - rolled up, but I think he must be seeing things.

N: At Ibstock? No, it wasn't there when we left. We had it down because we had fifty seats on the stage for Bingo. Ibstock was built as a theatre not a picture house and for live entertainment had a large stage and dressing-room in the early days.

A: We needed seats on the stage otherwise we couldn't get them all in.

B: Where did you call from?

N: The middle of the stage. They all sat behind me.

A: Those on the row immediately behind were on the look out for what was coming out. I'll tell you something that happened one night. As I've said, the car-park at the back belonged to the brewery, but we had the same right of way to it as the 'Ram'. It was a gorgeous summer's evening and we had all the double-doors open, so you could hear every sound. The whole thing was nice and airy. While everyone sat there playing Bingo, I went out and on to the car-park. A car had had its four wheels taken off and it had been stacked up on bricks. Even with the double-doors in the wall open, we had no suspicion.

N: The ground where they parked the cars was lovely and grassy in 1958 and those who had drunk too much in the pub would be lying out there, baking in the sun, since dinner-time.

J: Yes, it used to be the cricket ground in the summer and the fairground in October and later at other times. When the soundtrack of the film went quiet the traction-engines could be heard throbbing as they generated power for the roundabouts and lights.

Presenting The Palace Past

A: It used to be nice when the fair was there, but after the houses were built the fair went elsewhere.

N: Somebody took a picture of our last night there, when they were all coming out.

A: I don't know who has it.

B: We must try to find out. Thank you both for all your help. It has been most interesting.

The Palace as a Bingo Hall c 1980 (Photo: Mark Warner)

Presenting The Palace Past

Maureen Hunter Talks On Tape

My name was Maureen Satchwell. I lived in Gladstone Street with my mum and dad and I have a brother named Michael. My father used to work at the Palace, as the cinema operator, showing all the films for all the people in the village. I remember, when I was about eight years old, going along with dad to the Palace to help clean the picture house, putting all the seats back up and sweeping up.. It was a good time and I loved it very much.

I can also remember that dad used to make the slides to advertise the coming attractions. They were pieces of glass, which he white-washed, then printed the coming attractions for the following week to be projected on to the screen. At night he would bring them home and my brother and myself would wash them ready for the next show. It was a good time.

On one side of the Palace were windows, where you could see dad showing the films. Dad would open the window and I would say, 'What film are you showing today, dad?' He would open the box of the projector and the film would be projected onto the 'Ram' wall. Although it was upside-down you could still make out what was showing.

By the way, dad wasn't in the picture house on his own. My uncle, Mr Jim Satchwell, used to work with him. He was a character he was. Dad and Uncle Jim didn't just show films, they did the cleaning and made the fire in the boiler and kept it stoked with coke to keep the Palace and underneath the stage warm, particularly in the winter time. I've been there and watched it being made up on lots of occasions. I thought it was a fascinating place.

Presenting The Palace Past

I think everybody had a good time. It was one of the main attractions in the village. A visit to the cinema was something that everybody looked forward to - especially the children to the matinees.

We had a lot of fun there. At the kiddies' matinees all the children would be screaming when the films were on. I think a lot of people in the village will remember. Later on in the year the fair used to come to the village. Everybody went to the pictures first, then they came out to spend a little time round the fair before going home.

I don't think people realize how difficult it was being the cinema projectionist. At the end of a show dad had to rewind all the reels because at night time or the next morning he had to pack them up into steel boxes. Later a gentleman would come and pick them up and take them to the next picture-house. Films usually travelled on a regular circuit.

I can remember some of the tales dad used to tell. On the stage years ago there used to be performances of plays of some description. Also, he used to say that the Palace was haunted, I don't know how true that is - we'll never know. But these were the tales I liked to hear about. It was a good thing when you were off from school, you liked to enjoy yourself and to be with dad was always special anyway. He was a good guy. His and Uncle Jim's hard work provided the people in the village with somewhere to go because Ibstock wasn't a very big place when I was a little girl. We did enjoy ourselves and there was always something to do. I'm sure the children of today are missing out.

If you ever go to Ibstock and look at the Palace you will see that there are three entrances. One on the left, one in the middle and one on the right. The one on the left was for the

Presenting The Palace Past

lower paid seats, the one in the middle for the higher paid seats and the one on the right was used as an exit for people who had paid for balcony seats. From the balcony a staircase ran down the back of the cinema, but I don't think many people used it.

My brother and I didn't have to pay anything. We used to have complimentary tickets because of dad working there, which was really an added bonus.

Dad also had to organise the music that was played. In the projection box there was a music box, a kind of gramophone, on which he used to play old 78's as people were coming in and probably in the middle. He played the National Anthem at the end. Well, they were supposed to stand up for the National Anthem, but some people had buses to catch and would rush out.

I told you about the Palace being haunted. Before I close, there is this story that my dad told me. I'd be about 15 years old. He told me that my Uncle Jim and Mr Harry Flamson decided to stay in the Palace overnight to see what was actually going on. Between 1.00am and 2.00am.the seats that were normally raised began to go up and down on their own. The staff chairs were re-positioned, the door to the offices opened and shut and the locks were turned by invisible hands. At the time, they were the only two men in the Palace - so very strange. It was very brave of my uncle and his friend to stay that night in the Palace. I don't think that I would have liked that.

Dad also told me about once when they were lighting the fire Uncle asked dad to pass him the matches, which were on a shelf behind the door. Dad picked up the matches to pass to James. Uncle turned round to take the matches, but the matches had gone. They both looked at one another as if to say 'What on earth happened there?' This was another strange happening in the picture house.

Every so often a visiting variety group arrived to entertain the people of the village. Once they had lost a policeman's helmet, which was a property for one of the shows. It was found hanging from the stage roof. How it got there nobody seemed to know as there was no ladder in the village long enough to reach.

These are some of my memories of being a little girl in Ibstock. The Palace was a good place and I wouldn't like to see it pulled down. I would like it to be restored as a picture house or something for the village people to enjoy, because there's not a great deal of entertainment in Ibstock. Although it's quite a pretty place, people now have to go out of the village for much that used to be available in the past.

We've had our ups and downs in many things…… but I'll always remember the Palace.

Joe Satchwell

Presenting The Palace Past

Memories Are Made Of This by Barbara Webster

Yippee - it is Saturday, no school for two days. Hopefully I'll be going to the Palace this afternoon. No, not Buck House, just the 'Chicken Run' of our local cinema. Rich folk could afford to go in the 'Hen Roost' at night and pay more than a shilling for the pleasure but we were happy to go in the bottom entrance with a penny to hand over for admission. The penny - that was necessary - had to be earned.

Early every Saturday morning I'd nip off to a near neighbour and collect her order book. Off to the Co-op I'd go thinking 4840 - her Co-op number. The order book deposited at the bacon counter, I waited, sometimes patiently, for one of the men at one of the little sections of the counter to shout, '4840.' I'd go to the appropriate spot to find several items, bacon, cheese, lard and butter, already there. A huge sheet of brown paper would be laid out and the groceries assembled thereon. String would be hanging from a reel above and the final tying and knotting would see me on my way. My penny was safe.

However, it would be extra nice to feel I could nip into Mrs Moreton's sweet shop, which stuck out from the cinema, and buy something to suck. This meant another trip for a neighbour on the other side. 5072 was duly called after the book had been dealt with at the bacon counter and before long I was trudging down Chapel Street with my second burden.

Some folk would call at Baker's on the corner of New Road (Central Avenue) for a large bag of monkey nuts in their shells. I still recall the crunch under foot as we trooped out after the show. Others would save their penny for a bag of chips at the other Mrs Moreton's. A three-cornered bag which let you suck the vinegar from the lower part was everyone's delight.

I recall some of the stars we used to think were not really human. Alice Faye of the rich husky voice, which contrasted so much with Sonja Henie. We envied her as she glided across the ice. Will Hay and the unruly kids at school, Jesse Matthews with the kiss curls, Bette Davis, Merle Oberon and George Formby - magic. I can't remember who starred, but *The Mark of Zorro* left its mark on all of us.

Mind you, this was after the memorable day when Mr Ball came in front of the screen and said we were to go home and tell our parents that we could not get in for a penny next week. This was greeted with loud boos. It was going to cost twopence. Further loud boos. But the pictures were going to talk - loud cheers.

Mr Ball tried to separate the girls from the boys by putting a rope down the centre of the block of seats [4], but it was easy enough to be the first in the row and go and sit next to the rope. My boy friend at the time brought a pen knife and cut the rope each week till it was given up as a bad job and disappeared. Very little more than hand holding happened as we were too thrilled with the pictures.

I remember talk of Larry Gains, a famous boxer, fighting there - but I didn't see him. I did, however, go to see the selection of the beauty queen or carnival queen as she was called. Politicians used the building to try to persuade people to vote for them. I remember singing as we skipped:

---

[4] Councillor Don Costello and Mr Don Middleton confirm this anecdote.

Presenting The Palace Past

'Vote, vote, vote for Mr Morgan
Who's that knocking at the door?
If it's Harcourt Webb we will
Hit him on the head and he
Won't come knocking anymore.'

In later years I became one of the rich folk and paid one shilling and nine pence to sit in a double seat on the balcony for the first house on Saturday night.

I sincerely hope the re-birth of the Palace becomes a reality.

'Very little more than hand holding happened...'

Norman Tomlin
The Battram Boys

When I was six years old, my dad got the job as undermanager at Nailstone Colliery. So, my family moved from Moira into 'The Villa' at the top of Battram Road and my brother, Fred, and I became Battram Boys.

Every week we had our jobs to do for our mam. One would sweep the yard and swill around the bins while the other cleaned all the knives and forks. The following week we'd change over chores.

Although we had our work to do, we also got treats too. Mine was to join the bigger lads as they walked across the fields to Ibstock with a penny for the pictures and a penny for sweets in my pocket. We were heading for the Saturday matinee at the Palace. However, getting there wasn't always easy! As we got near to 'School Fields', the older lads would form up on the outside of the gang to give the younger ones some protection, just in case the Ibstock lads appeared with fists up and a challenge of 'I'll offer ya out!' It seldom led to a real fight but the Ibstock lads had quite a reputation for being a tough lot in those days. Looking back, I think it all added to the excitement and fun of the expedition.

One of the films I remember especially seeing was *Elmo, King of the Jungle*. It was one of my favourites. The Saturday matinee at Ibstock Palace was good entertainment and I guess it got me out from under my mam's feet for a couple of hours.

Anne Mears
On Call

During the war, my dad was a colliery electrician at Bagworth pit. He worked long hours and, along with other electricians, he had responsibility for making sure the machinery kept running night and day. Even when he'd finished his shift, he would also take his turn 'on call', and that proved to be a bit of a problem.

In 1939, when my parents got married they set up life together in Ibstock, where my mum had started her own hairdressing business, Now it looked as though they might have to move to Bagworth so that dad could get to the pit quickly when needed in emergencies. Fortunately a solution was found: we had a telephone installed and dad just had to be prepared to pedal as fast as he could on his push bike when a call came.

Did this mean no trips to the Palace to see the favourite films of the day? No. A quick word to the lady at the village telephone exchange and another word at the box office made sure mum and dad got an enjoyable night out, seeing the glamorous Hollywood stars and keeping up with the news and the latest fashions.

Occasionally, however, the precious evening out was cut short. And it must have been very frustrating when the film was interrupted and the following message flashed onto the screen - 'Mr Tomlin is needed at the pit'!

Paul Smith's Memories

The first thing I remember about the Palace is the physical structure. I was born in 1959 opposite the cinema at 12 High Street, in what is now a part of Hall's electric appliance shop. I remember the building always being white, with a black chimney cover, which turned with the wind direction. Before starting school, while my grandmother was looking after me, we used to sit in the front room (only used for special occasions). She once convinced me that we had seen a flying carpet come over the top of the Palace. I tell my children the same story, but neither of them believes me!

Stuck onto the front of the Palace, where the bus-stop is now, was Moreton's sweet shop, which jutted out to the edge of the pavement. (I have some home-made 8mm film showing Moreton's shop and the Palace front around 1963-64.)

It is difficult to remember what films I saw. *Snow White and the Seven Dwarfs* comes to mind and *The Fantastic Journey* with two dogs and one cat. One film I definitely went to see was, I think, a sex educational film - the name of which I can't remember. It was the talk of the play-ground both before and after the film. On seeing the lady have the baby, one lad had to rush to the toilet.

At the main entrance you bought your ticket, pushed aside the red curtain which stopped any light passing through during lights out, and stepped into the theatre. Once inside, a man would rip your ticket in half and, if the film had already started, a lady with a torch would show you to your seat. The same torch would be used to point you out if you were doing anything wrong or making a noise. At the end of the film you would file out through the nearest exit. For me this would normally be the large door to the left of the screen, which led out near to the chip-shop next door.

I even got into the picture house free one night when Arthur Brown, our next-door neighbour, let his daughter Julie and myself in through the back door and smuggled us upstairs into the balcony. Arthur helped out sometimes, together with his sister's son who helped to run the Bingo.

Behind the Palace was a very busy place. Holland's Fair always made camp there until the land was sold for building. The two Holland twins would come to play whenever they came to the village. I also remember a circus pitching its big top there once.

Elsie & Gordon Smith's Recollections

There were two entrances to the Palace. The entrance next to the chip-shop was for the cheapest seats where children would queue for the Saturday matinee. The other entrance was for the more expensive seats.

During the silent films, Alty Adcock would accompany the film on the piano. Alty lived just down the street at his own sports shop, which is now closed.

The films were shown by Jim 'Shine' Satchwell. One film that we remember was *The Face at the Window* starring Emlyn Williams.

One day they held a 'Bonniest Baby' competition, with photographs taken inside the Palace. Because we did not have any photographs of our twin daughters, Elsie took them over. The photo shoot was just inside the main entrance with boards erected as a back drop. Payment was up-front and I suggested that would be the last we saw of our money. To my surprise the photographs arrived. I think Edna Branson's daughter won a prize in this competition. We were so pleased with the photographs that we decided to have more copies. Again, payment was up-front. Only this time nothing happened. The man did a 'runner' with everyone's money. I believe he was eventually caught in another village.

Margaret Bills née Adcock
Remembers Her Courting Days

My dad went to Ibstock pictures twice a week; it did not matter what was on. When *Birth of a Baby* was on, my son wanted to go. I didn't know whether it was that children under fourteen or under sixteen had to go with an adult. My dad took him. I suppose my dad slept through it - he usually did, because when we asked him if the film was good he never seemed to know.

My husband and I did our courting at the pictures. We used to sit in double seats at the back   There was a space behind these seats and Mr Ball, the manager, used to walk along there and shine his torch on us to see what we were doing. Before we went into the pictures we went to Cyril Greasley's shop[5] to buy a bag of monkey nuts. We used to throw the shells over the back of the seats and when Mr Ball came along we could hear them crunching under his feet and know that he was on his way.

He always called Mr Satchwell, the projectionist, 'Shine'. There were two doors: one at the top and one at the bottom. Mrs Maud Clark sold the tickets at the bottom door and her husband, George, ripped them in half when you went in. Mr Ball's wife sold tickets at the top door.

There used to be crowds of lads who came from Hugglescote, Nailstone, Bosworth and Barton in the Beans so that we had to queue to get in.

---

[5] Across from the Palace, almost on the corner of High Street and Chapel Street.

Frieda Tabener née Eliffe
The Palace Cinema Remembered

Saturday night was always a special night of the week when I was little. This was the night when Dadda always used to take my Mum and me out. Where to? Well, where else but the magical cinema, the one and only Palace at Ibstock. I remember the crowds milling around outside, waiting for the first house to come out, queuing almost across the road, boys and girls eyeing each other appreciatively or not as the case may be. I was too young to be one of them, but the atmosphere was electric for we all wore our best clothes and made an event of the evening.

It was an especially important night for me, as I had to decide what my treat was to be for that week. The choice was: my pocket money (one hexagonal three-penny coin), or a tube of Smarties from Mrs Collier's sweet shop, or a banana from my Mum. What a decision! Mrs Collier was a lovely, almost shy, lady, who always made me feel so grown-up as I asked her for my tube of Smarties.

The night I remember most - not with regret, but sadness for my parents - was when I learned, sometime later, that my wonderful Dadda had taken us to the cinema on that fateful Saturday night instead of having his weekly 'two bob' on Littlewoods Pools. He couldn't afford both that week, and the line that he had chosen won; it was enough to have paid off the mortgage to his house. It seemed like a fortune to lose and money was scarce in those days.

Before I was old enough to be taken to the evening performance, I was allowed to go to the 'two-penny rush' on Saturday mornings when loads of children used to rush into the dimly lit cinema, Mr Clark keeping an eagle eye on the lads and Mrs Clark sitting behind the little window taking the money. I didn't believe that she was a real person, although I knew she was as she lived near to me. Mr & Mrs Clark were part of the fabric of the cinema, not entirely real any of it, a flight of fancy, the magic of the cinema.

As the programme started, all the children stamped their feet on the floor and cheered. If the film broke down, which it often did, the noise was deafening. Afterwards the lads used to rush out into the day-light, slapping their back-sides, rushing down the High Street; they were all the Hero of the cowboy film they had just seen; all were riding their 'horses'. What innocent fun, and they actually enjoyed it. No-one was *bored* in those days.

As the village boys and girls grew into young adults, many a kiss was stolen on the back row of the stalls and relationships which blossomed at the Palace probably still endure today. There was no television in those days so we got dressed up, communicated and mixed with our friends. It was an occasion that we looked forward to. Happy Days.

Two Of Alan Matterson's Memories

The Bell Push

By 1941 the war had truly come to Ibstock. The mines had been in full production since early in the previous year and most people, including women, were working long hours in the factories or on the land. Many, like my father, used to go off once or twice a week after work to act as ARP wardens or to serve in the Home Guard. The shops had little to sell, food and clothes were rationed, and virtually everyone travelled by bus when they needed to go to Coalville or Leicester. These were, I suppose, the golden days of the Palace for nearly everyone in the village went there once, or sometimes twice, a week. The programmes, always a double bill with a Gaumont British News (usually a couple of months out of date) and a Three Stooges shortie or a cartoon, included films that, at best. had first been shown on general release in the previous year, or so it seemed. Even so, the Palace knew its audience and few weeks went by without it showing a George Formby, a Frank Randle or an Old Mother Riley to pull in the crowds.

My father, an aficionado of Old Mother Riley films, took the whole family (Mum and the children, two boys and a girl) to the Palace to the second house one Saturday in 1941. He had booked five seats, in the front row of the balcony—the place to be—and we all sat there in a row waiting for the music to begin and the curtains to part. I sat at the end by the wall, next to my father, while my brother and sister sat on the other side of my mother, an arrangement which kept the troublemakers, my brother and I, well apart. Well, we sat there and waited. I became restless, as did most of the audience, and in Ibstock that always led to cat calls, to a few friendly fights in the wooden seats at the front of the stalls and to the beginnings of 'Why are we waiting?'

It was then that I noticed the bell-push. The fights were becoming serious by now and the cat calls louder. 'Why are we waiting?' had swelled into a rumbustious chorus when I pointed out the bell-push to my father.

'...I think the usherette presses it,' I asserted confidently, 'to start the films when all the seats are full, but she's not here tonight!'

'How do you know?' he asked disbelievingly. He always disbelieved me, I never knew why, and my mother burst in to say what she usually did:

'Oh Ala-a-a-n...' she said, as if I was already well on the way to damnation.

'I'm going to push it!' I yelled over the increasing tumult and reached up and pressed the button.

'Alan's pressed the button...' my brother pointed out in case my misdemeanour had been overlooked and my sister, who was only six, burst into tears.

'You shouldn't have done that Alan...' said my father sternly and my mother added: 'Wait till we get you home!'

And then, like magic, the music began and the curtains opened and I knew, instantly, that single-handed I had started the cinema programme by pressing that button. I was swollen with pride, but only for a moment for I spent the rest of the time fearful of a heavy hand seizing my collar and dragging me off to the police station for interfering with the cinema's arrangements. When the programme was over I hid behind my father and slunk out of the cinema and did not fully recover until we were safely walking home towards Station Road carrying packets of hot fish and chips.

I had never much liked Old Mother Riley films but that one incident put me off them for good.

Presenting The Palace Past

Belsen and Buchenwald

My friend Jim and I used to go to the Palace together quite often and, in late 1945, we went there midweek to see a Frank Randle film. It was unbelievably funny and the whole of the packed cinema rocked with laughter for nearly two hours. As the film came to an end we were both poised for the start of the National Anthem, the starting gun for the race to leave for the street, when to our astonishment the lights went up and a podgy man in a dinner jacket stood on the stage. Dinner jackets were not exactly common in Ibstock, any more than they are today, and that alone gave us pause.

The manager/owner of the Palace, for it was he, told us that there was an additional short film that evening. The film, he told us, had been made by the Crown Film Unit and the Government had asked all cinemas to show the film daily for at least a fortnight.

'...Anyone', he went on, 'of a squeamish disposition would be well-advised to leave but the Government considers that everyone should see the film if they possibly can...'

There was a brief interval to allow the squeamish to leave but hardly anyone did for few people in Ibstock were prepared to be considered squeamish. A buzz of conversation, mingled with cat-calls, had broken out but an unearthly quiet developed as the film began. We were watching, we realised, the appalling scenes in Belsen and Buchenawald, the concentration camps liberated by the British army, and the silence in the cinema became intense, palpable. No-one moved, no-one coughed and no-one cried, though we all wished we could. What we were seeing—images that have now been seen so often that they have lost their capacity to shock—were awful, horrific beyond imagining or understanding, and certainly beyond tears.

Frank Randle was in the distant past and we were all suddenly alone, wrapped in our own thoughts as we stared at those dreadful images on the screen. I had known, of course, that the Nazis had persecuted Jews, Gipsies, Communists and Socialists, indeed anyone who opposed the regime, but I had not known that it was like this, that the Nazis and the many who had helped them were evil creatures of the darkness.

The film came to an end. There was, I think, no National Anthem and we all filed silently and separately into the street. Outside there was usually a flood of noise and a rush to the fish and chip shops but not tonight. Everyone remained silent and hardly anyone spoke. None of us, in fact, wanted to do anything but go home. Jim and I walked down to where he lived and it was an effort to say 'goodnight' to him before setting off myself to go on my way. Most of the way home, along Station Road, was dark, unlit by street lights, and I could see those figures from the cinema, emaciated and skeletal shapes against the blackness, as I walked.

And I have never forgotten what I saw that night at the Palace.

Presenting The Palace Past

Jim Vaughan's Memories

(When I deposited my early memories, under the title *Coalslack and Custard,* in the Ibstock Time-capsule and Leicestershire Record Office, I had no wish to embarrass either living people or their relatives. To protect the innocent - as they say - people and places were given fictitious names, but lists of the real names of people and places alongside their fictitious names were provided on condition that they would only be available when the Time-capsule is opened, which, I was promised, would be fifty years hence, but is now likely to be a mere twenty. Here I have devised a different way of hopefully ensuring anonymity.)

Tarzan

One Saturday a Tarzan adventure had excited the children in the 'Chicken Run'. As Dorothy Lamour's Jane, secured to a stake set in a hole and buried up to her knees, tossed her head from side to side to avoid the native's blade threatening her throat, Tarzan struggled against the rope which bound him to the trunk of a tree. With the sheer power of his stomach muscles and only in the nick of time did he manage to separate the fibres of the rope, free himself, and rush to the damsel's rescue. The imaginations of our gang were inflamed and in our minds our bodies were pumped up like the muscles of our hero. To the general disappointment we quickly concluded that there was no chance of persuading any girl we knew to play the part of Jane.

To re-enact the inevitably abridged episode, we hastened to one of our dens under a young ash tree, growing with several others among a thicket of Snowberry bushes that lined Locker's Lane as it sloped down to the ford. Daddy Harratt, the headmaster of the County Junior School, called them Symphoricarpos albus, but children called them Snowberries, because towards the end of the summer the bushes would be covered with small white globes, far bigger than the pink flowers hardly noticed earlier in the year. Generations of Ibstock's children had picked the white globes to throw down to hear them pop underfoot. Behind the bushes was an abandoned lane-garden. Within this hideaway the members of a varyingly-constituted gang, all regular patrons of the cinema, attempted to emulate Tarzan's latest portrayal. Even though our gang used raffia-rope, which had secured orange boxes in one of the greengrocery shops, we only succeeded in making the skin of our bellies sore and proving the superiority of Tarzan's muscles. Someone suggested that perhaps the rope used in the film had been partially severed in advance, but that was heresy. Sadly we realised that our heroine would have perished.

The Price of Fame

How cinematic effects were achieved began to obsess us boys. One day we were standing on the steps of the Palace; *The Tudor Rose* was showing that week. We were grumbling that the trailer had failed to show any of the decapitations which from our sketchy outline of English history we felt to be essential. Number One, led on by Number Two, argued that the scene of the execution of Lady Jane Grey must obviously have been shot last.

'So yer reckon they chopped off the actress's head for real, d'yer?' I ventured.

Number Two said, 'She'd want paying a lot, wouldn't she, Jimmy?'

Number One took the bait, 'Yeah, if they'd paid her enough.'

'Don't be bloody daft!' called someone from the pavement. 'Nob'dy ud 'ave their 'ead chopped off for money, not even for five hundred quid. 'Ow could they spend it?'

'Then yo tell us 'ow they did it,' returned Number One in a huff.

That was a question I had been pondering, so I said, 'Yo'll 'ave to wait till Sat'day to find out.'

With Saturday and the all too slow flashing of each *'O' new reel marker,* our excitement mounted. At last, as Lady Jane walked to the scaffold, the parboiled whites of eyes and gaping mouths were all that the proprietor could see of the invisible-black tension that could be felt in the 'Chicken Run'. A timid voice breathed, 'She used to live at Bradgate Park,

Presenting The Palace Past

'She'd want paying a lot, wouldn't she?'

Presenting The Palace Past

'....stampeded out before the National Anthem.'

didn't she?' Perhaps its frightened owner felt that Bradgate was too near for safety. Jane's slim neck was exposed before she knelt. With no more concern than if she were about to be given a shampoo, she placed her chin upon the block. The camera followed the rising axe. It paused, then fell. Cannons spoke and their firing filled the screen and our ears. A fluttering cloud of pigeons rose. From their midst zoomed the caption: *The End*. For a moment there was a communal gasp then bedlam was let loose.

'Cheats! The rotten cheats!' shouted Number One.

'Weren't even any blood,' jeered someone behind us.

'Bloody rotten swizz!' came from a chorus of voices as their owners, slamming up the wooden seats as they left, stampeded out before the National Anthem began.

The British Legion's Gala Parade
Fancy Dress Competition

When Dad erred through ignorance, or misunderstanding, or as a result of one of his foibles, his in-laws, the Baylisses, chorused that he should have known better.

Only the day after the Fancy Dress Gala Parade was it discovered that Dad had blundered. Contestants were entered, prior to the day, into various categories, and Dad was charged with paying the fee and entering me as 'Sunny Jim'. The traveller of one of Mum's wholesalers had arranged for an outfit to be loaned from the makers of the breakfast cereal 'Force', and the thought of appearing as 'Sunny Jim' made me feel that I too could *leap high o'er the fence*, though no particular fence was specified in the advertising jingle.

The afternoon began with minor vexations and intimations of disappointment to come. The white trousers were a perfect fit and the spats clean out of my little world. The yellow waistcoat and red tailcoat were well on the way to incarnating the leaping figure of the 'Force' box, when the tall, white hat with its broad, black band, that should have emerged from the hamper clean-cut like a pill-box, was seen to have a two-inch brim. The 'real Sunny Jim' wore at the back of his head an upward-curving braid or plait rampant which a hat-brim would have impeded. Even without the brim, the limp skein of thick wool, attached to its mouse-coloured skullcap, could no way be induced to stand erect.

'There's nowt we can do,' said Dad.

'You'll have to make the best of it,' said Mum. 'Worse things happen at sea.'

I looked in the mirror and my face fell. 'The letters are back to front!'

My parents burst into peals of laughter. Mum took off the hat and held it for me to read. On the black band were the words 'Sunny Jim'.

'You silly dunce,' pealed my sister Mary, 'even I knew looking-glasses did that.'

I pouted. 'So did I. Just forgot.'

I was in an altogether better mood when I set off, right-gloved hand gripping the ashplant almost as tall as my hat and left clutching my entry card. Judging was to take place on the Palace stage. Awaiting their turn, competitors were seated in categories, for each of which three prizes were being offered. I found that in my group there were only three entrants, so that a prize for all seemed assured. I knew my rivals. Cousin Jean Foster had already won many prizes around the district in a Milkmaid outfit, designed by Uncle A. C. Foster to extol the virtues of his Jersey milk and cream. Mum's girlhood neighbour, Meg Knifton (née Tyler), had decked out her children and half those of West Walk as 'The Old Woman Who Lived in a Shoe'.

Soon I found myself waiting centre stage between Jean and the Kniftons. The judges, behind their table, seemed to be in some kind of difficulty until one of them discarded the third prize certificate. As the first prize card was pinned on to Jean's dress and that for the second prize on to the Old Shoe Woman's, I felt myself begin to blush. I was baffled, just as were my friends among the spectators of the Procession as it wound its way through the village streets to the Gala field.

'Yo should'a easily a won,' shouted Number One, coming across the grass for a closer inspection. 'Bloody judges!'

'The beggars don't know what they're doing,' agreed Number Two.

'Yer can say that agen!' urged Number One, as several girls in our class came to render mock admiration.

I was embarrassed. 'Me Dad entered me in the "Original Class" and "Sunny Jim" ain't original.'

'Oh, aren't we smart?' giggled the daughter of one of Dad's cousins.

Two girls from 'the bottom section' of our class passed sheepishly, followed by a girl I liked, who said, 'Jimmy, you do look nice.'

A girl that I liked even more scoffed, 'What, with that stupid thing sticking out at the back of his head?' I looked at my shoe and sniffed.

Humiliation on the Palace stage left me with no regrets when 'Sunny Jim'- along with a small charge for cleaning and a declaration that nothing had been damaged - was back in his hamper awaiting collection.

The Dance of the Seven Veils and Dark Eyes of London

I must have led a sheltered childhood for I was naïve when it came to attributing more than a *Boys' Own* kind of sinister motive to Bela Lugosi's abduction of lovely Greta Gynt, over whom he was leering before attempting to drown her in a large water-tank in his Thames-side warehouse lair. The film was *Dark Eyes of London*.

Greta, whose role as a British secret agent in *Crooks' Tour* had been much discussed by the lads in my class, had inexplicably made my knees go weak. In that film, watched by Basil Radford and Naughton Wayne who were sitting in a Near Eastern nightspot where she was engaged in discovering the identity of an enemy agent, she had performed an innocuous rendition of 'The Dance of the Seven Veils'. The two Englishmen. behind their copies of *The Times* were so concerned about the outcome of *The Test* that they barely noticed a later performance in which Greta's partner took hold of the edge of her wrap-around skirt, pulled, and twirled her like a spinning top across the dance floor as yards of her skirt unwound, exposing her frilly knickers.

I cannot be sure whether *Greta Breaks All Records* was the headline of a magazine publicity article or the in-your-face punch from the screen of the film's trailer, but the story was that during the filming of the disrobing scene Greta had crashed into a pile of records and bruised her comely thighs.

This long-legged beauty was now at the mercy of the Hungarian actor, who had bound her wrists and was hoisting her up towards the water-tank. The hero had been delayed, but was on his way as Greta wedged the heel of her shoe against the top of the tank. As the heel began to break away and her plight became desperate, the hero burst into the room. Greta was dropped unceremoniously to the floor. A bare-knuckled fight began and ended only when Bela, thrust backward against the double doors through which many of his victims had been thrown, fell into the tidal mud of the river. He struggled frantically, but the mud sucked him down until only his head and arms were visible. As he sank to his doom, the mud poured into his screaming throat and then he was gone.

The next night as I lay in bed, listening to the crowds from the cinema hastening to collect their fish and chips from Moreton's, Chaplin's, or Smith's, I pondered upon how many of the previous evening's patrons of the Palace, while walking home greasy-fingered, had reflected upon Bela's fate. When they had heard behind them a slow *clop-clop-clop and swish swish-swish,* few would have failed to recognize the advance of the horse-drawn *night-soil* cart.

GRETA BREAKS ALL RECORDS...

'...the filming of the disrobing scene....'

[6]Mrs 'Bid' Wilson née Ethel Spencer
Writes from Harlow

When I lived at 126, High Street, Ibstock, my name was Ethel Spencer. I have been known as 'Bid' since 1941 and Wilson since 1943. For several years my friend, Edith Sutton, has kept me up to date with Ibstock news and it was she who persuaded me to make a contribution to this book. My freelance writing has already included an article for *The Grapevine*.

My most single vivid recollection of the Palace is of that particular aroma of orange peel and Jeyes Fluid. When *The Grapevine* published a playbill from the nineteen-thirties it depicted a film I've never forgotten seeing there: *High Society Blues*, with Charles Farrell and Janet Gaynor. The theme music was *Just Like a Story Book*. At that time seating comprised of wooden forms with backs in the Penny Rush, and in the Tuppeny Rush wooden tip-up seats. The Balcony was mostly occupied by courting couples at evening performances.

I vaguely remember being given 2d to spend, but - being the devious character I am - spent 1d at Moreton's sweet shop and, praying that I didn't arrive home with nits, the other in the Penny Rush. My mother would have scalped me and grounded me for a month.

In the late nineteen-twenties we used to have a short annual season of a visiting variety troupe. Does anyone else have memories of this? Edith does because we have discussed it. The artistes were lodged around the village.

---

[6] Unfortunately this could not be found.

Presenting The Palace Past

In early nineteen-forty Bernard Newman gave a talk at the Palace - one night only - on how local troops were faring with the B.E.F. in France. Little did we know that, three months hence, Dunkirk was just around the corner.

Many people of my generation will recall how in the 'silent days' Alty Adcock bashed out appropriate music on the tinny piano. As Pearl White was about to be run over by a train, Alty's music reached a loud crescendo. The train approached - then - *To be continued next week.*

A Delve Into The Leicester Mercury Archives.
Extracts from The Mercury Campaign of 1995 in Support of the Conversion of the Palace.

Joe Satchwell
Based on an interview with Gill Smith: 24th November 1995

At the age of twelve, Joe Satchwell began his career in the cramped projection box at the back of the auditorium. Joe's uncle Jim, known as Shine, was the projectionist and Joe helped him by rewinding the films. Although the Palace was unheated except for two stoves, at seventy-nine, Joe, who lives in Gladstone Street, admits that those early days spawned his life-long love of the cinema.

'It's hard to describe,' he said. 'To see this crowd in front of you, to fade out the music and dim the lights was an amazing feeling. It was my life in those days. I'd watch the same film over and over again.'

Later, Joe became a professional projectionist at the Palace. He reckoned that the audiences of the early days were often less refined than the cinema-goers of today.

'When there was a cowboy picture the kids would be slapping their thighs. They'd throw orange peel and some would even bring their bows and arrows with them. At the end of the film the audience would stand up and applaud. The only time they knew we were there was when something went wrong. If a film stopped they'd start stamping their feet.'

The arrival of the first talkie at the Palace in 1931 was a milestone in Joe's life and the life of the village. The film was entitled *High Society Blues*, starred Charles Farrell and Janet Gaynor.

Joe is all in favour of transforming the derelict building into a multi-purpose arts centre for the locality.

Alty Adcock: Father and Son.
Based on an anonymous report: 30th November 1995.

This report states that seventy-nine-year-old Alty Adcock has vivid memories of his countless visits to Ibstock Palace Cinema where his father was the pianist.

One evening the film broke and the place was plunged into darkness. Eight-year-old Alty was thrust onto the stage by his father and told to sing. 'My dad stood me up on the stage and someone shone a spotlight straight on me,' he recalls. 'I could sing a bit and I even got a bit of a cheer. My moment of glory was short lived. My mother was annoyed with dad for letting me sing with dirty knees.'

Jessie, a ten-year-old village girl, who was in the audience that evening was destined to become Mrs Adcock. She vividly remembers how he climbed onto the stage and sang his heart out.

The Palace was a central part of Alty's childhood, for he spent many nights alongside his pianist father, who provided the music for the silent pictures. 'I used to carry my father's music so I could get into the films free' he said. 'He didn't really seem to use the music though. He would just play to the mood of the film and create sound effects, such as the beat of horses' hooves in cowboy films.'

'The Palace was part of our lives then,' he said. 'It only cost a penny to get in and it would have cost us sixpence to travel to Coalville.'

Presenting The Palace Past

Alty and John Snagge (Source unknown)

Alty senior was a keen pigeon fancier, who was once interviewed by John Snagge. Alty junior was a keen cricketer. His wife remembers how, when they were courting, she used to reserve one of the double seats on the back row. 'Alty would usually be playing cricket,' Jessie said, 'so I'd sit there on my own until he appeared. He'd usually turn up at about 9.30.'

The couple firmly support plans to restore the Palace to community use. 'I'd like to see it back in use,' said Alty. 'It would be nice to see films back there again. It would really make a difference to Ibstock.'

Commemorative Plaque.
Report dated 6th February 1996.

A Commemorative Plaque has been awarded to the Palace Cinema, Ibstock in recognition of its services in bringing entertainment to generations of local audiences. Only a few venues in the East Midlands have been honoured by Cinema 100, the London based organization set up to celebrate this year the centenary of cinemas in Britain.

The Inscription:

'The Palace Cinema, Ibstock. Founded c.1909.(sic)
Recalling with happiness and pride the pleasure
this cinema has given the Ibstock community.'

Appendix

STATUTORY RULES AND ORDERS
1930 No. 361
CINEMATOGRAPH, ENGLAND

REGULATION, DATED JUNE 6, 1930, MADE BY THE SECRETARY OF STATE UNDER THE CINEMATOGRAPH ACT, 1909 (9 Enw. 7 c. 30).

In pursuance of the Cinematograph Act, 1909, I hereby make the following Regulation:—

The Regulations, dated 30th July, 1923 (a), made under the Cinematograph Act, 1909, shall be read as if for Regulation 3 there were substituted the following Regulation:—

3.—(a) In order to secure the safety of the audience the licensee or some responsible person nominated by him in writing for the purpose shall be in charge during the whole time of any exhibition and he shall be assisted by a sufficient staff of attendants who shall be specially instructed by the licensee or such responsible person as to their respective duties, in particular in relation to the carrying out of the requirements of these Regulations.

Where at any exhibition the majority of the persons attending are under fourteen years of age the number of attendants required by the foregoing paragraph shall be such as to enable them effectively to control the movements of the children whilst entering and leaving the premises and during the exhibition and to ensure the orderly and safe clearance of the hall in case of emergency.

All the attendants shall remain on duty during the whole time that the premises are open to the public.

(b) All persons responsible for or employed in or in connection with the exhibition shall take all due precautions for the prevention of accidents and shall abstain from any act whatever which tends to cause fire and is not reasonably necessary for the purpose of the exhibition.

The licensee or the person nominated by him in writing as aforesaid shall see that the operators and every other person who may be called upon to handle inflammable film within the building for any purpose are fully instructed as to the dangers arising from the use of inflammable film, the precautions to be observed to prevent risk of ignition and the steps to be taken in the event of a film smouldering or catching fire.

This Regulation shall come into operation on the first day of July, 1930.

J. R. Clynes,
One of His Majesty's Principal
Secretaries of State.

Whitehall,
6th June, 1930.

(a) S.R. & O. 1923 (No. 983) p. 111.

LONDON: PUBLISHED BY HIS MAJESTY'S STATIONERY OFFICE
To be purchased directly from H.M. Stationery Office at the following addresses:
York House, Kingsway, London, W.C.2; 13a Castle Street, Edinburgh, 2;
39-41 King Street, Manchester, 2; 1 St. Andrew's Crescent, Cardiff;
Tower Lane, Bristol, 1; 80 Chichester Street, Belfast
OR THROUGH ANY BOOKSELLER

1948
(Reprint)
Price 1d. net

Presenting The Palace Past

On the previous page is a scan of a Document found in Archives of Ibstock Historical Society.

As can be seen, the copy is so damaged as to be almost illegible. The Editors tried to obtain a new copy from HMSO, which has been so fragmented that the quest became a mammoth task, taking us eventually to the British Library Out of Print Documents Department. All that could be purchased - for a fee of £7-50 - was a photocopy of the entire fifteen pages of the 1948 Revision of the original 1923 Regulations as amended on 6th June 1930. The cost of the document shown on the previous page was one old penny and is reproduced here as it casts light on Mr Ball's insistence of good behaviour in the Palace.

Opposite is a reproduction of a 1948 Reprint.

STATUTORY RULES AND ORDERS
1930 No. 361
CINEMATOGRAPHY, ENGLAND
STAFF

3. (a) In order to secure the safety of the audience the licensee or some responsible person nominated by him in writing for the purpose shall be in charge during the whole time of the exhibition and he shall be assisted by sufficient staff of attendants who shall be specially instructed by the licensee or such responsible person as to their respective duties, in particular in relat'on to the carrying out of the requirements of these Regulations.

Where at any exhibition the majority of the persons attending are under fourteen years of age the number of attendants required by the foregoing paragraph shall be such as to enable them effectively to control the movements of the children whilst entering and leaving the premises and during the exhibition and to ensure the orderly and safe clearance of the hall in case of emergency.

All the attendants shall remain on duty during the whole time the premises are open to the public.

(b) All persons responsible for or employed in or in connection with the exhibition shall take all due precautions for the prevention of accidents and shall abstain from any act whatever which tends to cause fire and is not reasonably necessary for the purpose of the exhibition.

The licensee or the person nominated by him in writing as aforesaid shall see that the operators and every other person who may be called upon to handle inflammable film within the building for any purpose are fully instructed as to the dangers arising from the use of inflammable film, the precautions to be observed to prevent risk of ignition and steps to be taken in the event of a film smouldering or catching fire.